ROCKCLIMBING

BY HOLLIE ENDRES

BELLWETHER MEDIA • MINNEAPOLIS, MN

Are you ready to take it to the extreme? Torque books thrust you into the action-packed world of sports, vehicles, and adventure. These books may include dirt, smoke, fire, and dangerous stunts. WARNING: read at your own risk.

This edition first published in 2008 by Bellwether Media.

No part of this publication may be reproduced in whole or in part without written permission of the publisher. For information regarding permission, write to Bellwether Media Inc., Attention: Permissions Department, Post Office Box 1C, Minnetonka, MN 55345-9998.

Library of Congress Cataloging-in-Publication Data
Endres, Hollie J.
  Rock climbing / by Hollie J. Endres.
     p. cm. -- (Torque : action sports)
  Includes index.
  Summary: "Amazing photographs accompany engaging information about rock climbing. The combination of high-interest subject matter and light text is intended to engage readers in grades 3 through 7"--Provided by publisher.
  Includes bibliographical references and index.
  ISBN-13: 978-1-60014-127-0 (hardcover : alk. paper)
  ISBN-10: 1-60014-127-7 (hardcover : alk. paper)
  1. Rock climbing--Juvenile literature. I. Title.

GV200.2.E53 2008
796.522'3--dc22   2007019868

CONTENTS

REACHING THE TOP

A climber clings to the side of a tall cliff. He slowly and carefully moves up the rock face. A rope anchored into the rock is all he has to protect him from a dangerous fall.

He presses his fingers into tiny dips in the rock. He rests the tips of his toes on small bumps called footholds. He throws his legs over and pulls himself up. He can't wait to reach the top and take in the beautiful view.

fast fact

Rock climbing originated in Europe in the 1880s.

WHAT IS ROCK CLIMBING?

Rock climbers use skill, strength, and simple tools to scale cliffs and mountainsides. Rock climbing is dangerous and exhausting work. Climbers love the challenge of a tough rock wall.

fast fact

To "campus" in rock climbing means to climb using only your upper body.

Climbers use **anchors** to secure ropes as they climb. They **rappel** to get down to the bottom after a climb. Some rock climbers think rappelling is almost as fun as climbing.

Climbers rely on **harnesses** and ropes. Harnesses connect climbers to their ropes. Ropes help them climb and protect them from falls. Most climbers use **dynamic ropes**. These ropes are stretchy. They do not snap if a climber falls. Ropes are linked to anchors and harnesses by metal clips called **carabiners**.

Anchors connect the rope to the rock. A **piton** is a type of anchor that is jammed into a crack in the rock. Other types of anchors include nuts, cams, hexes, and bombers. Climbers choose their anchors based on the type of rock they are climbing.

Other gear is important to safely enjoy a
climb. Tight-fitting climbing shoes give a climber
the best possible grip on the rock. Hand chalk
soaks up sweat from a climber's hands.

There are many styles of rock climbing. Top-rope climbing involves a climber and a **belayer**. The belayer stays at the bottom holding the climber's rope tight. The rope runs from the climber through the anchor and back down to the belayer. The belayer pulls the rope to keep it tight.

There is no belayer in lead climbing. Two people climb at the same time. The leader climbs a section of rock and anchors the rope. The partner follows. Only one climber moves at a time. The lower climber uses the rope to catch the leader if they fall.

Rating System

In the United States, climbers use a standard rating system to describe the difficulty of different routes:

• **5.0 through 5.4 — beginner level**
Easy to climb, like a ladder.

• **5.5 through 5.7— intermediate level**
Climbable in normal shoes or boots but requiring more skill.

• **5.8 through 5.10 — experienced level**
Requires climbing shoes, experience and strength.

• **5.11 through 5.12 — expert level**
Perhaps only the top 10% of climbers in the world can handle these routes.

• **5.13 through 5.14 — elite level**
Can only be handled by the best of the best.

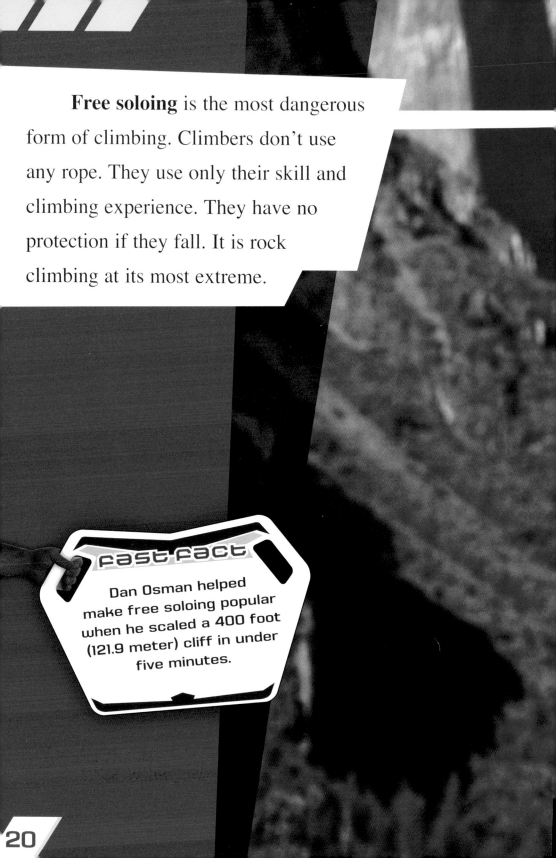

Free soloing is the most dangerous form of climbing. Climbers don't use any rope. They use only their skill and climbing experience. They have no protection if they fall. It is rock climbing at its most extreme.

Fast Fact

Dan Osman helped make free soloing popular when he scaled a 400 foot (121.9 meter) cliff in under five minutes.

GLOSSARY

anchor—a device that secures a rope to a rock face

belayer—someone on the ground who holds a climber's rope tight in top-rope climbing

carabiner—a metal clip which connects the ropes to harnesses and anchors

dynamic rope—rope that can stretch

free soloing—rock climbing without ropes

harness—a set of straps worn by a climber that connects to the rope

piton—a peg driven into a crack used as an anchor

rappel—to make a vertical descent down a rope

TO LEARN MORE

AT THE LIBRARY
Deady, Kathleen W. *Extreme Rock Climbing Moves*. Mankato, Minn.: Capstone Press, 2003.

Jefferis, David. *Rock Climbing and Mountaineering*. Austin, Tex.: Raintree Steck-Vaughn Publishers, 2002.

Seeberg, Tim. *Rock Climbing*. Chanhassen, Minn.: Child's World, 2004.

ON THE WEB
Learning more about rock climbing is as easy as 1, 2, 3.

1. Go to www.factsurfer.com
2. Enter "rock climbing" into search box.
3. Click the "Surf" button and you will see a list of related web sites.

With factsurfer.com, finding more information is just a click away.

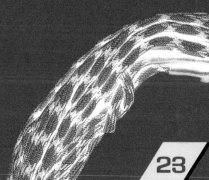

INDEX

The photographs in this book are reproduced through the courtesy of: Brad Wrobleski/Master File, front cover, pp. 5, 10-11, 16; Vasilly Ganzha, p. 3; Nathan Bilow/Getty Images, pp. 4, 15; Karl Weatherly/Getty Images, pp. 6-7; Joe Gough, p. 8; Greg Epperson/Getty Images, pp. 9, 12-13; Hermann Erber/Getty Images, p. 14; Andrew McGarry/Getty Images, p. 17; Juan Martinez, pp. 18-19; Patitucci Photo/Getty Images, pp. 20-21.